free
refill

An 8-session Bible Study by

mark atteberry

Discussion Guide by
jon weiner

Standard®
PUBLISHING
Bringing The Word to Life
Cincinnati, Ohio

free refill

Group Member Discussion Guide

Published by Standard Publishing, Cincinnati, Ohio, www.standardpub.com.
Copyright © 2007 by Standard Publishing. All rights reserved. No part of this book may be reproduced in any form, except for brief quotations in reviews, without the written permission of the publisher.

Free Refill, ISBN 0-7847-1912-8, text © 2007 Mark Atteberry

Written by: Jon Weiner
Project editor: Michael Mack and Margaret K. Williams
Cover design: Studio Gearbox
Interior design: Edward Willis Group, Inc.

All Scripture quotations, unless otherwise indicated, are taken from the Holy Bible, *New Living Translation,* copyright © 1996. Used by permission of Tyndale House Publishers, Inc., Wheaton, Illinois 60189. All rights reserved.

ISBN 978-0-7847-1992-3

13 12 11 10 09 08 07   9 8 7 6 5 4 3 2 1

CONTENTS

Introduction 7

SESSION 1:
Refilling Your Faith in His Understanding
John 4:5-30 11

SESSION 2:
Refilling Your Faith in His Presence
Matthew 14:22-33 15

SESSION 3:
Refilling Your Faith in His Words
Matthew 8:23-27 and Mark 4:37-41 19

SESSION 4:
Refilling Your Faith in His Promises
Luke 5:1-11 23

SESSION 5:
Refilling Your Faith in His Love
John 13:1-17 27

SESSION 6:
Refilling Your Faith in His Goodness
John 11:1-44 31

SESSION 7:
Refilling Your Faith in His Victory
John 20:1-18 35

SESSION 8:
Refilling Your Faith in His Return
Matthew 24:3-14, 36-44 and 1 Thessalonians 4:13-8 .. 39

How to Use This Guide

This guide is designed for group use with the companion book, *Free Refill*. It will help your group discuss the ideas from *Free Refill* and apply them in your lives. This happens best in groups that are growing together in real friendships, real faith, and even real fun!

True to the Bible

The aim is not to study a book, however. It is to study God's Word, using *Free Refill* as a launching pad. We have designed this guide, like all the Standard Publishing products you've come to trust, to be true to the Bible.

True to Life

We designed this guide also to be true to real life—life in the real world of spouses, kids, jobs, bills, and other everyday circumstances. We want this guide to help your faith intersect with real life, so you will live the life that Jesus promised: life to the full!

A number of features make this guide distinctive:

- *It is designed for busy people.* You will not need to spend hours preparing for meetings, whether you are the leader or another member of the group. At the same time, reading the companion book, *Free Refill*, is highly recommended to help you get the most out of this study.
- *It is designed for people at various maturity levels.* You do not need to be a Bible scholar to facilitate or participate in these studies. The companion book will provide the "teaching" each week. Your job is to discuss and apply the truths from God's Word to your lives.

- *It is designed to develop community.* Your group—whether you are a Sunday school class, Bible study, or small group—will grow closer to one another as you share your stories, study the Word, and serve together. The optimal number of participants in a group is usually about three to ten, depending on a variety of circumstances. But larger groups can still be very effective. We suggest you subgroup if your group is larger than twelve. You may want to break into several groups of three to six during the Study and Apply sections, for instance, for deeper discussion and more authentic application.

- *It is designed to help you grow spiritually.* Real, lasting life change is the primary goal. The Holy Spirit will transform you as you allow him to work through God's Word and other group members to encourage, support, admonish, and pray for one another. Your group will employ Colossians 3:16: "Let the word of Christ dwell in you richly as you teach and admonish one another with all wisdom."

How Each Session Is Organized

Leader Preparation: Use this section to prepare your heart and mind for the meeting. To maximize opportunities for spiritual growth in your group, take time to read and reflect. Also, use this time to pray for group members.

Bible Study Agenda: This is an inductive rather than deductive study. It is designed to help participants *discover* truth from God's Word through group interaction rather than just *telling* them what it says. It is also designed to help participants observe, contemplate, wrestle with, and take action on Scripture. Use the questions to facilitate lively interaction among group members. This will lead people to "aha" moments—when they "get it." Ask follow-up questions to keep a good discussion moving. Keep the group on track with strong yet gentle encouragement and guidance.

For the Leader

You are in a vital position to help people grow in their relationships with God. The best leadership comes out of the overflow of a godly leader's heart. The "Leader Preparation" section and other leader helps are included to feed your heart first—to equip and encourage you before you lead your group. God has called you to shepherd this small group of people that he has entrusted to your care. We want to provide whatever support and resources we can to help you carry out this vital ministry to which God has called you. See the article from www.SmallGroups.com in the Appendix to help you grow as a spiritual leader and shepherd.

- *Connect:* Utilize the Connect questions to help group members share about what they know best—themselves—and get them actively involved in the discussion. The main question here is, "What is *your* story?"
- *Study:* These discussion questions are arranged to help members first observe and examine the Bible text, then understand and discern what the Scripture means and how they relate to it personally. The question here is, "What is God saying to you in this passage?"
- *Apply:* This is the most important meeting element. Make sure you move the group toward this part of the process. Here they will relate God's Word to their own everyday lives and decide what they will *do* with it. The question here is, "How will I respond?"

Before the Next Meeting: Encourage group members to read the next chapter in *Free Refill* for the upcoming meeting. They may also look up Scripture passages if they like, but they do not need to do any "homework" other than what's listed here.

Leaders Between-Meeting Shepherding Ideas: A healthy, life-changing small group is more than just a once-a-week meeting. Set an example by staying in contact with participants between meetings though phone calls, visits, email, and personal letters or cards. The best groups are like close families that care for one another 24-7.

Refilling Your Faith in His Understanding

"But the water I give them takes away thirst altogether. It becomes a perpetual spring within them, giving them eternal life."

—John 4:14

The goal of this session is to help you understand that through faith in Jesus we can find answers to life's deepest thirsts, struggles, and disappointments. Everyone has problems that arise in life. Finding solutions can become a huge task. In his encounter with a Samaritan woman, Jesus teaches us that his grace and peace are free gifts for our good, if we will look toward the Source.

Leader Preparation
- ❏ Read John 4:5-30.
- ❏ Read the introduction and chapter 1 of *Free Refill*.
- ❏ As you begin this study, how are *you* being refilled, leader? Be prepared to share how God is working in you as you prepare for this study of his Word.

CONNECT

1. When you were a child, what did you want to be when you grew up? What happened to that dream?

> There are in fact two words that, when spoken together at just the right moment, have amazing, life-changing power. No, they're not "magical" in the Harry Potter, wand-waving sense. But make no mistake, these two words have been known to breathe new life into wheezing, withering souls. They've been known to lift burdens, calm fears, and inspire hope. Timed right, they are as refreshing as a cold front in July. I'm referring to the words, "I understand."
>
> —*Free Refill*, p. 15

2. Who in your life really knows you well? How well do they understand the issues that concern you?

STUDY

Read John 4:5-30.

She came to the well alone, which was a subtle but clear indication that she had few, if any friends. In those days, fetching water was women's work and they happily turned the task into a social event. Their evening walks to the well (which was about a half mile from the village) gave them a welcome break from household chores and a cherished opportunity to catch up on the latest gossip. The only reason a woman would go to the well alone in the scorching midday heat was if she didn't fit in or wasn't welcome with the rest of the girls.

—*Free Refill*, pp. 18, 19

3. Put yourself in the Samaritan woman's sandals for a moment. What do you imagine she was thinking about as she made her way to the well that day?

4. Jesus began the conversation with the woman by asking her for water. What are some of the concerns raised by this request?

5. How would you characterize the woman's response to Jesus after hearing his offer of *living water* (v. 15)?

6. What purpose did it serve to have the woman tell her story concerning her current life situation?

> **Leader's Note**
> The well, known as Jacob's well, was located in Shechem, an ancient altar site important to followers of God. Sychar was near this important place. This well is fed by underground springs. Because the water is moving and not from a reservoir, it was called "living water." Jesus gave a new meaning to this term.

APPLY

7. Take 20-30 seconds to think about a time when you had a powerful encounter with someone who really challenged you to think *outside the box*. How did that encounter make you feel? What did you learn from the experience?

Volumes have been written about the things Jesus said to this woman. In particular, his comments about worshiping in spirit and truth are considered foundational. But to fully appreciate Jesus' compassionate understanding, we must give some thought to what he didn't say. He didn't enumerate her sins, lecture her for setting a bad example, ask for an explanation, demand an apology, or tell her she was going to hell if she didn't shape up. It's hard to imagine a preacher standing face to face with the biggest sinner in town—a woman whose life would have made a great Jerry Springer episode—and not even broaching the subject of morality, but that's what Jesus did.

—*Free Refill*, pp.19, 20

8. What do you learn from Jesus about how to approach people with tangled lives who consistently make bad choices?

9. Mark Atteberry mentions that Jesus was tempted in every way, just like each of us. Hebrews 4:15 says that Jesus "understands our weaknesses, for he faced all the same temptations we do, yet he did not sin." What encouragement does this passage give you, knowing that Jesus understands your weaknesses?

Many people are confused, alarmed, or worried about their inability to stay on the straight and narrow. Even the apostle Paul said, "I don't understand myself at all, for I really want to do what is right, but I don't do it. Instead, I do the very thing I hate" (Romans 7:15).

—*Free Refill*, p. 22

10. What are some ways we as a group can support one another as we walk through life together?

Before the next meeting:
   ❏ Read chapter 2 of *Free Refill*.
   ❏ Think about how your relationship with Christ has changed your life. Will you share some of this at the next meeting?

Refilling Your Faith in His Presence

"But Jesus spoke to them at once. 'It's all right,' he said. 'I am here! Don't be afraid.'"

—Matthew 14:27

The goal of this session is to help us remember that the Lord is near and that he knows our deepest needs. This session challenges us to see Jesus even in the most desperate storms of life. No matter how strong we believe we are, Jesus is stronger. He is the master of the wind and waves . . . and our lives as well.

CONNECT

1. What is one reason you have for praising God this week?

> ➤ *Leader:* When everyone has had an opportunity to share, take a moment to pray, thanking God for knowing our needs and hearing our prayers.

2. Last session ended with a simple request to reflect on how your relationship with Christ has changed your life. Who would like to tell your story?

3. What is one challenge you have had to face "head on"? How did it turn out?

Leader Preparation

- ❑ Read Matthew 14:22-36.
- ❑ Read chapter 2 of *Free Refill*.
- ❑ As you read this chapter, apply it to your own life first. What elements or enemies are you facing head on? In what area of your life has Jesus been telling you, "It's all right. I am here! Don't be afraid"?

STUDY

Read Matthew 14:22-36.

4. Imagine we are Jesus' disciples in this story. Let's walk through the account, and for each part, discuss what each of us would be sensing and feeling:

➤ Jesus sends us to the boat to cross the lake

➤ The winds pick up and waves buffet the boat

➤ In the storm, we see someone (or something?) walking on the lake

➤ We hear Jesus say, "It's all right. I am here! Don't be afraid"

➤ Peter walks on water . . . then begins to sink

➤ Jesus and Peter get into the boat and the storm dies down

5. If you had been on the boat, what would you have done in the middle of the raging storm?

❏ Given up and headed for shore

❏ Complained but carried on

❏ Encouraged everyone to keep rowing

❏ Prayed

❏ Other: _____

Leader's Note

To get the most out of this session, be sure to read the previous passage in Matthew, the account of Jesus feeding the 5,000 (14:13-21). Don't miss the point—that Jesus saw the need for food for the crowd. He provided the fish and loaves, and at the end left twelve baskets full, perhaps one for each disciple to remind them that he is worthy of our faith. Jesus knows our needs! In this study Jesus once again meets needs, and the situation is desperate, to say the least.

APPLY

6. Mark Atteberry says, "One thing is certain: feeling that the Lord is out of touch or out of reach is one of the most terrifying experiences a believer can have." (p. 32) When was a time you felt God was unreachable?

➤ What did you do about it?

When Jesus says, "Don't be afraid," he's meeting us at the point of our biggest weakness. He's challenging us to do something that goes completely against our nature. And he often forces us to wrestle with that challenge for a while by temporarily withholding his power.

—*Free Refill*, pp. 37, 38

6. Scan this list. Which do you fear the most?

- ❑ Failing my family
- ❑ Failing in my finances
- ❑ Failing at my job
- ❑ Failing my God

Why?

8. Atteberry writes that Jesus controls the "elements" and the "enemy." (p. 35) What elements or enemy are you facing right now?

➤ How does it give you comfort that Jesus is in control of both the elements and the enemy?

Jesus doesn't say, "Try not to be afraid." He says, "*Don't* be afraid." He lays it down as a command, knowing full well that our tendency toward fear is our greatest weakness.

—*Free Refill*, p. 37

9. Why do you think Jesus sets the bar so high?

➤ How do you think being a member of a small group helps to overcome fears?

10. Read this Bible verse out loud together:

"God is our refuge and strength, always ready to help in times of trouble."

—Psalm 46:1

Say the first name of someone you know who is facing a storm of life. Be sure to pray for them with your group.

Before the next meeting:

- ❑ Read chapter 3 of *Free Refill*.
- ❑ Reflect on the challenge Jesus offers when he says, "Don't be afraid." How can you encourage someone in your group with that message before the next meeting?

Refilling Your Faith in His Words

"The disciples just sat there in awe. 'Who is this?' they asked themselves. 'Even the wind and waves obey him!'"
—Matthew 8:27

The goal of this session is to help us understand that Jesus' word speaks with power and authority to answer our every need. But we need to have a desire to spend time in our Bibles if we ever want to find the security of those answers and the promises they offer.

Leader Preparation
❑ Read Matthew 8:23-27 and Mark 4:37-41.
❑ Read chapter 3 of *Free Refill*.
❑ Perhaps the most important role of a leader is modeling. How are you doing as far as getting God's Word in *you*?

CONNECT

1. Today's lesson centers around the power of Jesus' words. To begin, let's gather in a circle. Starting with me (the leader) each person will say one word or phrase that lifts up the person to your right.

> ➤ *Leader:* Close this time in prayer, acknowledging God's presence and power.

It's impossible to overestimate the power of words. They have the power to injure or heal, poison or nourish, deceive or enlighten, or save lives or cost them. It is no exaggeration to say that the course of history can be changed with a single sentence.
—*Free Refill*, p. 47

2. Tell about a time when you were healed or hurt by someone's words.

STUDY

Read Matthew 8:23-27 and Mark 4:37-41.

3. These are two perspectives on the same event. Compare and contrast them. What are some significant things you learn from one passage that are not in the other?

4. What do you imagine the disciples are thinking about as Jesus slept while the storm raged?

5. How do you relate to the disciples' distress when they cried out, "Teacher, don't you even care that we are going to drown?" (Mark 4:38)?

6. Why is it sometimes hard for people to believe that God can meet them in the midst of their storms?

APPLY

7. Who will share about a time when you were in a storm, and God seemed silent? How did that make you feel?

8. In Matthew 8:26, Jesus rebuked the disciples by saying, "Why are you afraid? You have such little faith!" How does regularly reading or listening to Jesus' words help people have faith in the midst of storms?

9. How has God's Word influenced you in times of crisis?

➤ How has it helped you lend support to others struggling in a storm?

Leader's Notes
One of the main teachings in the passages concerning Jesus calming the storm concerns his *authority* over nature. It was one thing to see Jesus healing, loving, and caring for people. It's another thing altogether to see him command authority over the wind and the waves. Don't miss the point here. Jesus is absolutely capable of handling every one of our problems, needs, and even our worst storms. And he does it with his words.

If your cup is running low on faith, you probably don't give as much attention to his words as you once did. Perhaps you can't even remember the last time you picked up your Bible, headed for a quiet spot, and started reading in earnest.

—*Free Refill*, p. 52

10. How often do you read your Bible? What gets in the way of your reading the Bible more often?

11. Is there a storm you are facing right now that seems beyond your ability to manage? Are you willing to talk about it and let us as a group pray with you about it?

Before the next meeting:

❏ Read chapter 4 of *Free Refill.*

❏ Schedule at least 2 or 3 times this week to get alone with Jesus and read your Bible. Share what you learned during the next group meeting.

Refilling Your Faith in His Promises

"And this time their nets were so full they began to tear!"
—Luke 5:6

The goal of this session is to help us understand that Jesus' words bring the promises of life. Through the efforts of a fisherman and his friends, we are once again reminded that trusting in God is always the right choice.

Leader Preparation
❏ Read Luke 5:1-11.
❏ Read chapter 4 of *Free Refill*.
❏ Life can disappoint us. So can people. What about God? Today's lesson centers on the promise of God that if we trust him, he will meet our deepest yearnings.

CONNECT

1. Last week's challenge was to spend some time reading your Bible. Is anyone willing to share your experiences with the group? What do you think God is teaching you through his Word?

2. Besides your parents or others who raised you, who is someone you really trusted as a child?

STUDY

Read Luke 5:1-11.

3. Look at verse 4, what might you have been thinking about Jesus if you were in Simon Peter's sandals?

4. Why do you think Simon Peter obeyed Jesus' request?

5. In what other ways did Simon Peter and the other fishermen respond to Jesus that day?

APPLY

The whole point of this miracle was to impress on them [the disciples] that he [Jesus] was someone who could be trusted. When he made a promise, they could count on it coming true.

—Free Refill, p. 65

6. What is one of the promises of God that you embrace, trust, and believe?

7. Is there a promise of Jesus that causes you to struggle in your faith? Why?

8. In Matthew 19:29, Jesus said, "And everyone who has given up houses or brothers or sisters or father or mother or children or property for my sake, will receive a hundred times as much in return and will have eternal life." When has your obedience to Jesus' words caused problems with family or friends? How did you resolve the issue?

9. What message do you send when you choose faith over feelings in decision making?

10. Peter was an experienced fisherman, yet he chose to go against conventional thinking to follow Jesus. Mark Atteberry states, "Our Lord's promises sometimes challenge us to go against the grain of our culture" (p. 70). What do you believe is the greatest cultural struggle of faith for young adults and families today? For those in midlife? For older adults? For you?

11. "Nothing will turn your heart cold and bitter like the betrayal of a loved one. The pain stems not just from the betrayal itself, but from the sudden fear that there's no one you can trust." (p. 74) Do you consider it a betrayal on God's part when he doesn't protect you from being hurt? Why or why not?

12. We all have times of doubt and struggle. What are some practical ways our group can support and encourage each other in the tough times?

> **Leader's Notes**
> Many of us have experienced failures of faith with devastating effect. The goal of this lesson is to remind group members that the message Jesus gives in his promises is that we matter to God. His desire is for us to rest in him *and* his words.

Before the next meeting:

- ❑ Read chapter 5 of *Free Refill*.
- ❑ Pray this week for strength of faith as you interact with your feelings, family, and our world's culture.

Refilling Your Faith in His Love

Leader Preparation
❏ Read John 13:1-17.
❏ Read chapter 5 of *Free Refill*.
❏ Sometimes it's difficult to understand God's love. The Bible clearly speaks of it, yet there are times when we just can't seem to believe it's true. In today's session we will study a significant moment in the life of Jesus and his disciples and will examine once again the love of God demonstrated by and through Jesus Christ.

"'No,' Peter protested, 'you will never wash my feet!' Jesus replied, 'But if I don't wash you, you won't belong to me.'"

—John 13:8

The goal of this session is to help us understand that Jesus' words bring the promises of life. Through the efforts of a fisherman and his friends, we are once again reminded that trusting in God is always the right choice.

CONNECT

1. Answer one of these two questions:

➤ Who is your favorite superhero? Why?

➤ When was a time you were really dirty? What caused you to get so filthy?

2. Can you recall a time when God didn't make clear sense to you? What were the circumstances?

STUDY

Read John 13:1-17.

3. What were the circumstances surrounding this event? Describe the scene and the atmosphere.

4. Why do you think Jesus chose this method of "teaching" his followers?

5. How would you characterize Peter's response to Jesus' actions?

> When Jesus gently lifted those ugly, stinking feet and rinsed and dried them with the loving care of a mother bathing her newborn baby, he was showing his disciples that he could stomach their filth. But not just that he *could* stomach it. He was showing them that he *would* stomach it.
>
> —*Free Refill*, p. 81

Leader's Note
There is an obvious correlation between the washing of the disciples' feet and the dirt and stain of sin upon our lives. You might have your group members read and dwell on these verses: Romans 3:23; 6:23; 8:1, 2; 8:28.

6. What is the difference between being *able* to do a difficult task and actually doing it?

7. How did washing feet express love for the disciples?

8. Mark Atteberry says, "Who would have dreamed that there was something more nasty and gross at that table than the disciples' feet? But there was, and it was Judas's heart. Imagine how awkward he must have felt when Jesus pushed the basin toward him and looked up into his eyes" (p. 84). Knowing what Judas was about to do, why did Jesus still wash his feet?

APPLY

9. Have you ever been in the position of serving someone who had wounded you deeply? How did you feel at that moment?

> ➤ What do you think God was teaching you through that time?

10. How might you have responded if Jesus was washing your feet?

11. What does the story of the foot washing teach you concerning Jesus' love for humanity? For you?

12. Is there an issue in your life over which you are wrestling with God? Will you share it with us?

Before the next meeting:

- ❏ Read chapter 6 of *Free Refill*.
- ❏ Before leaving, buddy up with another group member. Take a few minutes to schedule a time when you will get together with him or her to pray specifically for a personal struggle.

Refilling Your Faith in His Goodness

Leader Preparation
- ❑ Read John 11:1-44.
- ❑ Read chapter 6 of *Free Refill*.
- ❑ There are times when your group members struggle, wondering whether God understands their pains, failures, and battles. That's normal—for you as a leader as well. We need to be reminded often that God indeed understands, because he has been in our shoes. In today's lesson, you will read about a terrible pain in the life of our Lord, and perhaps get a clearer picture of his heart that loves us so.

"I am the resurrection and the life. Those who believe in me, even though they die like everyone else, will live again. They are given eternal life for believing in me and will never perish. Do you believe this?"

—John 11:25, 26

CONNECT

1. Answer one (or if you have time, two) of these questions:

➤ If you could rid the world of one fear, what would it be? Why is that fear significant to you?

➤ Have you ever had someone confront you to your face and tell you what a terrible person you were? Did you deserve the attack? Briefly share the story.

➤ Have you ever needed to comfort a grieving person? How did you feel in that situation?

❑ Awkward. I didn't know what to say.

❑ Uncomfortable. I'm not used to being in that kind of situation.

❑ Incompetent. I don't think I said or did anything that helped.

❑ Dispassionate. To tell the truth I didn't really feel anything.

❑ Blessed. It was a privilege to have God use me to provide comfort.

STUDY

Read John 11:1-44.

2. What words would you use to portray the situation in Bethany?

3. How would you describe Jesus' relationship with Lazarus and his family?

4. Jesus does not immediately respond to the news of Lazarus' illness, but waited two days. Why do you think he delayed responding to this crisis?

➤ What do you think Jesus did during those two days?

5. "I am the resurrection and the life." How would you put Jesus' statement into your own words?

Leader's Note
In the passage for this lesson Jesus is confronted by the painful loss of his dear friend Lazarus. But even through his pain, Jesus used the moment to teach the believers that nothing, not even death, can separate them from his love. Have the group read Romans 8:38, 39 together as a reminder of Jesus' eternal promise to believers.

APPLY

6. How is your faith bolstered by Jesus' statement?

7. Jesus performed a great miracle in raising Lazarus. How confident are you in his power to meet your greatest needs?

❏ Very confident—I have no doubts.

❏ Mostly confident—I have some struggles.

❏ Less than confident—I doubt he even hears me.

8. Mary and Martha were good friends of Jesus, yet they had to wait for him. Patience can be a hard lesson to learn. How difficult is it for you to wait on God?

9. Mark Atteberry writes, "I love the fact that he [Jesus] had a tender, breakable heart . . . that he was emotionally invested in the lives of his friends" (p. 102). What can you learn from Jesus' tears? What comfort, if any, do they bring?

10. Atteberry says, "So often we conclude that because he [Jesus] isn't *doing* anything, he must not be *feeling* anything. But nothing could be further from the truth" (p. 103). When was a time when you wondered if God cared about you? What was happening to you at the time?

> Right now, as you hold this book in your hand, you may be able to tell about a time when the Lord rescued you from a dark place.
>
> Or you may be trapped in a dark place at this very moment, wondering if it's really possible that you could finally be set free. Look at those three key words again: "Lazarus, come out!"
> Now, remove Lazarus' name and insert yours.
> Say it out loud.
> Say it again.
> Hear the Lord calling you to leave the darkness behind and step into the sunshine. He promised that captives would be released. There's no reason why you shouldn't be one of them.
> —*Free Refill*, pp. 104, 105

11. As we end our meeting, let's break into groups of two or three and discuss:

> ➤ This may not be easy to do, but would you be willing to step out of your comfort zone and talk about a dark place the Lord has rescued you from or that you are currently in?
> ➤ What do you experience when you hear Jesus say to you, "_____, come out!"?
> ➤ Conclude by praying for each others' needs in your subgroup.

Before the next meeting:

> ❏ Read chapter 7 of *Free Refill*.
> ❏ Is there someone in the group who is struggling with significant issues? Can you commit to pray specifically for those needs every day? Is there something more your group can do to support him or her?

Refilling Your Faith in His Victory

"'Why are you crying?' the angels asked her."

—John 20:13

CONNECT

1. How do you most like to express your love to people you care about?

- ❏ Touch
- ❏ Words
- ❏ Gifts
- ❏ Time with them
- ❏ Acts of kindness

2. When was a time when you felt totally hopeless? What brought you around? How long did it take?

STUDY

Read John 13:1-17.

The ultimate victory garden is the one Mary Magdalene entered with a heavy heart on the Sunday morning following Jesus' crucifixion. She hadn't just lost a friend or a loved one. She had watched the cruel murder of the one person who had done more for her than anyone else ever would . . . or could. Jesus had cast seven demons out of her, he had treated her with dignity and respect, he had seen her potential and cultivated it, and he had defended her when others criticized. Mary was a woman who'd grown accustomed to scorn and ridicule. At one time, she probably thought she'd never be treated

with such love and kindness. And now, with Jesus dead and buried, she surely believed she never would be again.
—*Free Refill*, p. 111

3. Mary was an eyewitness to the events surrounding Jesus' death and resurrection. As we look back at the passage and follow her through this account, let's describe from the passage what she observed with her five senses . . .

> ➤ as she went to the tomb "while it was still dark."

> ➤ the first time she was at the tomb but did not look inside.

> ➤ as she ran to tell the disciples.

> ➤ when she looked in the tomb.

> ➤ when she saw Jesus.

> ➤ when she heard Jesus.

4. Mary had the privilege of seeing the resurrected Jesus. He said to her, "I am ascending to my Father and your Father, my God and your God." How would those words bolster faith and strengthen hope?

5. When Jesus appeared before the disciples, he showed them his hands and side (v. 20). How would it benefit the disciples to see his wounds?

> ➤ How did they react?

APPLY

6. Mark Atteberry writes, "There are many times in life when a partial victory, though disappointing, is still better than no victory" (pp. 113, 114). What about Jesus' resurrection makes his victory complete?

I am deeply grateful to God that he accomplished the crowning work of his redemptive plan conspicuously . . . that he gave us lots of evidence, not just to bolster our faith, but to keep us from living with the gnawing fear that we're being hoodwinked.

—*Free Refill*, p. 116

7. Have you ever been afraid, even momentarily, that Christianity was the ultimate snipe hunt and that you were the butt of the joke? If so, what triggered that fear? How did you deal with it?

8. What facts give you the most assurance that the Gospel is true?

9. How has the resurrection of Jesus affected your life?

10. Who in your sphere of influence can you tell what you just told us? (As you close, be sure to pray for those mentioned, as well as for opportunities to tell them about Jesus.)

Before the next meeting:

❏ Read chapter 8 of *Free Refill*.

❏ Jesus doesn't just offer eternal life, he offers an abundant life here and now. Is there someone in the group that needs to hear the message of hope for today? Take a few moments this week to connect with those fellow group members and remind them of our victory in Christ!

Refilling Your Faith in His Return

"Let us not neglect our meeting together, as some people do, but encourage and warn each other, especially now that the day of his coming back again is drawing near."

—Hebrews 10:25

CONNECT

1. Do you ever worry when you hear predictions about the end of the world? Why or why not?

2. On a scale of 1-5, with 5 being very often, how much do you think about the second coming of Christ?

STUDY

Read Matthew 24:3-14, 36-44 and 1 Thessalonians 4:13-18.

3. Take a few minutes and summarize the teachings from these passages.

4. What are some specific ways a Christian can "keep watch" (Matthew 24:42)?

5. Jesus uses the examples of two men walking in a field and two women working in a mill, saying one will be taken and one left behind. What do you learn from this passage concerning Jesus and his return?

Leader Preparation

❏ Read Matthew 24:3-14, 36-44 and 1 Thessalonians 4:13-18.
❏ Read chapter 8 of *Free Refill*.
❏ The return of Jesus is a theme that resonates way beyond the church. From popular books and movies to doom-saying preachers, there has not been another area of Christianity that has created so much attention and controversy. A goal for this lesson is to focus on living an expectant life in Christ, looking for his return. Be careful not to get caught up in opinions!

APPLY

6. What do you think the dangers are, if any, of reading religious fiction dealing with end times, but not the Bible?

> Many people think of "Noah's day" as a time of decadence, and it was. But that doesn't seem to be Jesus' emphasis here. . . . Jesus' point seems to be that *good* people are going to be *preoccupied* and, therefore, unprepared for his return. . . . People . . . rarely think about the second coming. What they *do* think about is making the mortgage payment, picking up the dry cleaning, and getting the kids to their piano lessons on time. As one person recently said to me, "I want to do more for God, but *life* keeps getting in my way!"
> —*Free Refill*, pp. 131, 132

7. "*Good* people are going to be *preoccupied* and, therefore, unprepared for his return." Do you agree with this statement? Why or why not?

8. How does busyness affect your ability to be prepared for Jesus' return?

9. What keeps you trusting and believing in God even though it has been 2,000 years and Jesus has not yet returned?

10. How would knowing the time when Jesus is coming back make a difference in how you practice your faith?

11. What evidence in your life would indicate your readiness to meet Jesus?

12. What, if anything, do you think you need to do in life before meeting Jesus?

> ➤ What stops you from doing that now?

Leader's Note
In Matthew 24:36, Jesus says, "No one knows the day or the hour when these things will happen, not even the angels in heaven or the Son himself. Only the Father knows." Remind group members that God alone is in control of the return of Jesus. Many have tried and failed in their predictions. What a waste of time! Perhaps a better use of our time would be to pray for those who you know are not yet believers in Jesus. Can your group name folks that you can pray earnestly for as Jesus tarries?

Closing Remarks

➤ As you finish this group series, take time to review what you have learned together over the past eight sessions. Make a list of things you can celebrate that God has accomplished in your group. Then make a list of continuing prayer requests and distribute that list to all group members.

➤ Plan a meal together to celebrate the community of faith that you share in your small group!

Maintaining Spiritual Focus

by Rick Lowry

Small group leadership can be a detail-intensive ministry. Lesson preparation and regular contact with group members are hard enough to squeeze into a busy leader's calendar. Add to these the scheduling of hosts and refreshments, information updates, and attendance at training sessions, and it becomes one of the most demanding ministries in the church.

With all these elements to keep up with, it is easy to lose spiritual focus. Here are some ways that I, as a small group leader, maintain my spiritual focus.

GROWTH ATMOSPHERE. A small group leader can provide a positive atmosphere for spiritual growth. Above all else, my goal as a small group leader is the spiritual success of the individuals God has placed under my spiritual care. I am willing to do whatever it takes for the members to find God's will for their lives and to help them move in an upward direction. As their shepherd, I am coming to God on my knees and saying, "God, please give me insight into each person's life in my group, so I can determine what exactly they need in order to move to the next spiritual level."

BIBLICAL FOUNDATION. Spiritual leadership means making the Bible the foundation of group life. We rightly think of small groups as a tremendous relational opportunity. But as vital as relationship building is in small groups, the Word of God is still the foundation. It should be obvious to any visitor to our group meeting, any random week, that the Bible is essential to us.

PERSONAL HOLINESS. The most important thing I can do to lead my flock spiritually is to be spiritual myself. I cannot lead people to a place I have not been (or maybe even am not willing to go).

My daily prayer is "Lord, how closely am I walking with you?" I have developed ten questions to ask myself on a regular basis to make sure I am knowing God more deeply:

- Holiness: Am I progressively moving away from sin?
- God's Word: Is God's Word food to me, and am I spending time in it?
- Worship: Am I worshiping regularly, both privately and corporately?
- Sharing faith: Am I sharing my faith regularly?
- Stretching faith: Am I stretching my faith regularly, stepping out of my comfort zone to a place where I depend on God?
- Prayer: Am I daily talking and listening to God in prayer?
- Solitude: Have I been alone with God enough to hear his voice clearly?
- Serving: Am I serving with the abilities God has given me?
- Spiritual progress: Am I further along in my relationship with God than I was a year ago?
- Accountability: Have I made myself accountable to another trustworthy brother or sister for my spiritual maintenance and growth?

If I can answer yes to those ten, I can be fairly sure that I am putting myself in a place to know God more deeply with every year that passes. I can be confident that God can use my leadership to implant spiritual growth in my group members.

I have been to groups where people seem afraid to talk about spiritual things. Most people won't automatically gravitate toward spiritual concerns in a group discussion. They look to the leader to open the spiritual door and invite them in.

INTIMATE KNOWLEDGE. A spiritual leader knows his or her group members well. This takes time, building trust and expressing interest.

This knowledge begins with the little things. Do I have the birthdays of the people in my group on my calendar? Can I name their children? Do I know their struggles? Do I know how they best connect? Is she a studier? Is he a person for whom relationships are important? Which ones are oriented more toward feeling or thinking?

Jesus modeled a depth of care as he who lays down his "life for the sheep." When was the last time I made a sacrifice to see my group members grow in Christ—a sacrifice of time perhaps, doing a little extra preparation to give this week's lesson a creative edge? Or a sacrifice of energy to get them involved in a service project. A good leader knows the group members and chooses activities based on their spiritual needs.

VALLEY WALKING. A good leader walks with group members in their spiritual valleys. Romans 12:15 encourages us to "Rejoice with those who rejoice; mourn with those who mourn." That means we have taken the time to enter into the joys and pains of the life of another person, a vulnerable and risky business.

Members experiencing a spiritual valley will sometimes shy away from the group with whom they previously enjoyed fellowship. A wise group leader will go to them, offer assurance, and even help heal relationships that may be strained.

PRAYER AND DEPENDENCE. I will never experience any spiritual success if I attempt to lead my small group by my own power and wisdom. I must depend on God. I must pray daily and fervently for God to do his work among my group members. As I lead, I keep my eyes on Jesus. He went to the trouble of purchasing his people with his own blood. He will not refuse wisdom to those of us he has called to aid in the spiritual formation of his redeemed.

Reprinted with permission from www.SmallGroups.com.

FREE Small Group Resources

With the purchase of this book, you are entitled to a free 1-month membership at www.SmallGroups.com where you can get even more small group resources like this article. To claim your FREE membership:

- Go to: www.SmallGroups.com/freemembership
- Continue through "checkout" process
- Select payment method "check/money order." However, no payment is due if you use the coupon code: stdsgo6
- Then click "Redeem" and "Confirm Order" for your free membership.